PUFFIN POETRY

POETRY
Pie

ROGER MCGOUGH was born in Liverpool, and received the Freedom of the City in 2001. President of the Poetry Society, he presents the popular Radio 4 programme *Poetry Please*, and has published many books for adults and children. In 2005 he received a CBE from the Queen for his services to literature.

www.rogermcgough.org.uk

POETRY
Pie

ROGER McGOUGH

PUFFIN POETRY

PUFFIN BOOKS

UK | USA | Canada | Ireland | Australia
India | New Zealand | South Africa

Puffin Books is part of the Penguin Random House group of companies
whose addresses can be found at global.penguinrandomhouse.com.

puffinbooks.com

First published 2015
001

Text and illustrations copyright © Roger McGough, 2015

The moral right of the author/illustrator has been asserted

'Rhyming Sausages', 'The Juggler' and 'Skywriting' first appeared in
It Never Rains, published by Penguin Books 2014

Set in Baskerville MT
Printed in Great Britain by Clays Ltd, St Ives plc

A CIP catalogue record for this book is available from the British Library

ISBN: 978–0–141–35686–0

www.greenpenguin.co.uk

dedication (dedikǎⁱʃən) *n.* complete and wholehearted devotion.

To those dedicated to poetry,
the writers, the readers, the spreaders
of the word, this book is dedicated.

Contents

The Arrow's Song

The arrow sang as it flew through the air:

'I'm free of the bow and I don't care

Where I land, what I hit, be it target or tree,

Flying through the air is the life for me.'

Excuses, Excuses, Excuses

I'm not making excuses, but I have to say
My journey here was a nightmare today
The riverbank burst and the streets were flooded
Trees sank to their knees and buildings shuddered

Traffic lights howled and pulled scary faces
Pillar boxes set off on cross-country races
Foxes hunted hounds and bit off their noses
While lamp posts held hands and played ring o' roses

Policemen and policewomen danced on the beat
A zebra crossing galloped off down the street
Beggars gave money to passers-by
There was an old lady who swallowed a . . .

Bicycles were chased and devoured by cars
Did I mention the invasion of monsters from Mars?
These terrible things all happened to me
On my way here to see you . . . Honestly!

Lame Excuses

'Sorry, miss, I sprained my ankle.'

'Sorry, miss, my sister kicked me in the shin.'

'Sorry, miss, the dog ate my walking stick.'

'Sorry, miss, my kneecap fell off.'

'Sorry, miss, I dropped a piano on my foot.'

'Sorry, miss, my crutches burst into flames.'

'Sorry, miss, there was a tarantula in my trainer.'

'Sorry, miss, an elephant stood on my toe.'

(Accidentally.)

Sound Advice

Never badger a badger in the dark
Or swing a tiger by the tail.
Never use a hammer-headed shark
For knocking in a nail.

Never be rude to a poodle
Or cook a cock-a-doodle stew,
Invite a grizzly round for a meal
In case he makes a meal out of you.

And never, but never . . .

1) Tickle piranhas

2) Put goldfish in the dishwasher

3) Play hoopla on a rhino's horn

4) Plug an electric eel into your guitar.

And never, but never, whatever you do . . .

Play hoopla with piranhas in the dark
Or swing a rhino by the tail.
Never use an electric guitar
For knocking in a nail,

Invite a badger round for a meal
Of eel and poodle stew.
Never be rude to a dishwasher.
All sound advice for you.

Quicksilver

Let your imagination
Feed on the fantastic
Let it move like quicksilver
Stretch like elastic

 Boring old classrooms
 Changed in a trice
 To a witch's kitchen
 A palace of ice

A steaming jungle
A distant planet
A silver spaceship
With you to man it

Your bedroom, a good room
You love it, but wow!
Now a sailing ship
With you at the prow

You're flying a jet
At five hundred plus
Or grabbing the wheel
Of a runaway bus

Let your imagination
Feed on the fantastic
Let it move like quicksilver
S-T-R-E-T-C-H - L-I-K-E - E-L-A-S-T-I-C

Loose Talk

If teapots could talk
They would tittle-tattle like mad
About tea things like teabags and teaspoons
And the wonderful teatimes they had.

If petrol pumps could talk
What stories they would tell
About oil and the price of diesel
But they can't, which is just as well.

If flowers could talk
How long before they'd sing?
The Blues in the cruel midwinter,
Hosannahs in the spring.

If bullets could talk
Wouldn't that be thrilling?
'Keep those guns away from me
I'm sick to death of killing.'

If the Earth could talk
It would make a terrible din
About the mess we humans
Have left the bathroom in.

If skeletons could talk
They'd rattle on every day
About clavicles and fibulas,
Ribs and vertebrae.

Until the sun goes down
And tired of talking bones
They'd jiggle on the dance floor
To the sound of xylophones.

The Power of Poets

The man sitting on the settee,
stroking a cat and watching TV,
isn't me.
I am the settee.

I could have been the man,
the cat or the TV.
However, this is my poem
and I choose to be the settee.
Such is the power of poets.

Rhyming Sausages

Sausages though tasty
Are difficult to rhyme.
Unlike pies
Which rhyme with skies, for instance.
And lies, and surprise and sighs
And capsize and flies and prize.
To mention only seven.

Bossages

Wossauges

Sausages, though tasty,
Are difficult to rhyme.
Unlike a pasty,
Which rhymes with nasty.
Oddly, it doesn't rhyme with tasty.

Zozziges

Sausages though tasty
Are difficult to rhyme
So I seldom eat them.

Quosages

The Game of Rhymes

Guess the missing rhyme. (Answers on page 104)

Steeples are too steep and bells are too ringy
Bees are too busy and wasps are too _ _ _ _ _

Jim is too grim and Becky's too bubbly
Your ears are too big and your knees are too _ _ _ _ _

The tiger is too stripy and the leopard too spotty
The collie is too Welsh and the terrier too _ _ _ _ _

Bears are too grizzly and kangaroos too jumpy
Moose too morose and camels too _ _ _ _ _

Geese are too greasy and pigs are too porky
Trumpets are too brassy and violins are too _ _ _ _ _

Tambourines are too hippy and banjos too twangy
Ghosts are too ghoulish and vampires too _ _ _ _ _

Tangerines are too pippy and cherries too stony
My favourite food is a plate of _ _ _ _ _

Take a Bow, Cow

Take a bow, cow.

You with the beautiful eyes.

Without you, there'd be no ice cream,

no Milky Way in the skies.

Without you, coffee and cocoa

would be undrinkable.

Imagine a world without MOO?

Unthinkable.

The Giant Panda is Having a Baby

There's panda-monium down at the zoo
As the heart-warming news filters through:

The giant panda is having a baby!
A baby, a baby!

The giant panda is having a baby!
Keep calm, keep calm!

The giant panda is having a baby!
A baby, a baby . . .

No she isn't. Sorry, false alarm.
(It's one of the zookeepers.)

The Bigger the Clog

The bigger the clog
The smaller the forest
The smaller the forest
The dearer the log

        The dearer the log
        The smaller the fire
        The smaller the fire
        The thinner the smoke

The thinner the smoke
The cleaner the air
The cleaner the air
The bigger the people

        The bigger the people
        The larger the feet
        The larger the feet
        The bigger the clog

The bigger the clog
The smaller the forest
The smaller the forest
The dearer the log.

RECYCLING

I care about the environment

And try to do what is right

So I cycle to school every morning

And recycle home every night.

Factory Facts

I work in a factory that makes factories.
We manufacture them intact.

I'm a factory factory worker
In a manufactory, in fact.

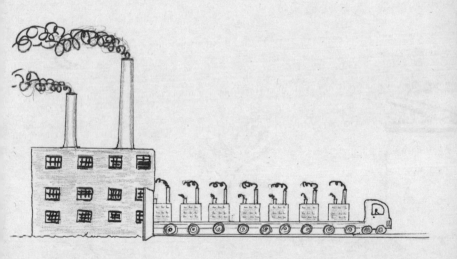

Mr Pollard

In the dead of last night
we had a visit from Mr Pollard.
With his giant scissors
he lopped the branches off the trees in our road.

Today, like teenagers with bad haircuts,
they stand, gawky and embarrassed.
Birds stay clear. The sun bides its time.

M.I.P.

The cat who always got the cream
Grew obese.
Died in early middle age.
May she Meeeow in Peace.

The Pimple Fairy

Years ago when in my teens
and happy as could be
I came out in spots.
Or rather, spots came out in me.

One day I had an ordinary sort of face
and the next, as if from outer space,
the aliens had landed.

Washed and scrubbed three times a day,
moisturised and toned it.
But those bullies swaggered around the place
as if they owned it.

Spent my pocket money on every gel and cream
but without success.
My face, let's face it, looked a mess.

Then one night, as in a dream,
the Pimple Fairy appeared,
her complexion smooth as petals on a summer rose.
Flawless (save for the boil on the tip of her nose).

The sight of me was enough for her
and taking pity on the plight of a fellow sufferer,
waved her wand and cast a magic spell
before bidding me a blemish-free farewell.

The spell worked, and in the morning not a spot.
My skin as smooth as a baby's bot.

So three cheers for the Pimple Fairy
on hand when the battle rages
to fight the dreaded zit,
The curse of all teenagers.

Missing Cat

'You've called having seen the poster

But it's not as simple as that.

To claim the reward on the offer

You must first hand over the cat.'

Fruity

Plums are plummy

Pears are peary

Peaches are peachy

Goosegogs are hairy

And pineapples?

The Lost Lost-Property Office

'On buses and trains you wouldn't believe
The crazy things that passengers leave:

A pair of crutches, I kid you not,
Hot-waterbottle, full but no longer hot

A bouncy castle deflating slowly
Glove discarded by a one-armed goalie

Pink chiffon tutu for a large ballerina
A can of worms and a concertina

A ventriloquist's dummy with nothing to say
An Egyptian mummy all dusty and grey

A scaffolder asleep in a Spider-Man suit
The tangled remains of a failed parachute

A Viking helmet and a broken lance
A pair of elephant's underpants

A file with **TOP SECRET** stamped in red
(Inside a card, *April Fool* it said)

An Alpine horn and a didgeridoo
A signed photo of Winnie-the-Pooh

A shot-putter's shot and a pole-vaulter's pole
Two Yorkshire puddings and a toad-in-the-hole

Headphones and hearing aids by the score
A mountain of mobiles and a lavatory door.

A bucket of toenails and a wooden plank
Two air-to-air missiles and a Russian tank

Lost any of these? Bad news I'm afraid,
The Lost-Property Office has been mislaid.'

Elephants and Peas

(and apes)

Elephants and peas have much in common:

Both are green
(Except elephants)

Both have tusks and long trunks
(Except peas)

Both roll off the fork
(Except elephants)

Both rhyme with 'smelly pants'
(Except peas)

Both are delicious, when mushy, with fish and
chips
(Except elephants)

Elephants and peas have much in common
(Both have apes in them).

Pineapple

Though as fearsome
as a hand grenade
A pineapple will quench your thirst

But before you take
a mighty bite
Make sure you peel it first.

The Town Crier

The Town Crier cried both night and day,
'Alas! My wife hath run away.
I am forsaken, I am undone,
For whom I tolled my bell hath gone!'

Oyez! Oyez! Oyez!
Boo hoo! Boo hoo! Boo hoo!

He burst into tears in the town hall square
And blubbered: 'My cupboard alas, is bare
No food for my childer, now cold winds blow.
Whither I goest, all is woe.'

Oyez! Oyez! Oyez!
Boo hoo! Boo hoo! Boo hoo!

He wrung his hands and he rung his bell.
Buckets of tears for the wishing well.
He wept, he whimpered, he snivelled, he groaned,
He wailed and whined, he howled and moaned.

Oyez! Oyez! Oyez!
Boo hoo! Boo hoo! Boo hoo!

With ears ringing and eyes full sore
The townsfolk they could stand no more:
'For crying out loud both night and day
We're going to send you far away.'

So they took his bell and his tricorn hat,
His scarlet coat and his deaf old cat
And drove him seven leagues from town
Where in the forest they set him down.

*   *   *

Did he drown in tears? Who can tell?
Or find a kind of peace at last?
Like echoes of a half-muffled bell
Two hundred years have passed.

The forest, now half its former size,
Remains three leagues from town
And be prepared for a ghostly surprise
Should you choose to venture down.

First light is the best time to be there
Before the bustle and throng
When the dawn chorus fills the air
And the woods come alive with song

And listening closely you might hear
Among the melodies, bright and clear,
A tearful refrain, a plaintive cry.
What bird would carry such sorrow, and why?

oyayoyayoyay

woo hoo, woo hoo, woo hoo

oyay oyay oyay

woohoo, woohoo, woohoo

oyez oyez oyez

Boo hoo Boo hoo Boo hoo

Easy Pickings?

You've got me to thank
Otherwise your face
Would be a pancake – blank.

Snub, hooked, I vary in size.
If you tell lies it grows and grows
Like Pinocchio's.

What am I?

A Good Listener?

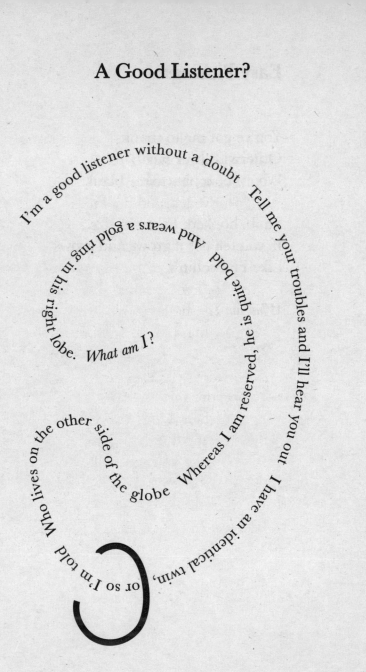

I'm a good listener without a doubt Tell me your troubles and I'll hear you out I have an identical twin, or so I'm told Who lives on the other side of the globe Whereas I am reserved, he is quite bold And wears a gold ring in his right lobe. *What am I?*

A Bouncer?

Toss me aside and
     I'll bounce back
At leaving no traces
     I've learned the knack

I'm a good friend
     but you couldn't care less
Never say thanks
     when I clean up your mess

You ignore me
     when things go well
But seek me out
     when you misspell.

What am I?

My First is in Apple

My first is in apple and also in pear
My second is in blond but not in fair

My third is in classroom and also in clock
My fourth is in dress but not in frock

My fifth is in England and also in France
My sixth in flamenco but not in dance

My seventh is in giant and also in ghost
My eighth is in honey but not in toast

My ninth is in italics and also in tail
My tenth is in jailer but not in gaol

My eleventh is in kitchen and also in cook
My twelfth is in library but not in book

My thirteenth is in mountain and also in climb
My fourteenth in nursery but not in rhyme

My fifteenth is in octopus and also in ox
My sixteenth in pyjamas but not in socks

My seventeenth is in quiet and also in queue
My eighteenth is in riddle but not in clue

My nineteenth is in sun and also in star
My twentieth in traffic but not in car

My twenty-first is in uncle and also in aunt
My twenty-second in vertical but not in slant

My twenty-third is in worry and also in woe
My twenty-fourth is in Xmas but not in snow

My twenty-fifth is in yeti and also in yet
My twenty-sixth brings an end to the alphabet.

What am I?

happle

unhapple

very unhapple

O is for . . .

o is for open sesame and over the rainbow

o is for open-hearted and open-minded

o is for orange and orangutan

o is for oceans to cross and opportunities to take

o is for oxygen, or 0^2 as it likes to be known

o is for ovation, you deserve it

o is for opticians if you can't read this

W is for . . .

wonderfully

weird ideas

like an escalator

up Mount Everest

for lazy mountaineers.

L is for . . .

L is for the Leather
That goes to make a shoe.
L is for the Limerick
'There was a young lady from Crewe.'
L is for the Leap
You make before you Look.
L is for the Letters*
That go to make a book.

*There are 38,734 in this one.
(Bet you can't count them!)

Countdown

This

short

poem

about the

importance

of mathematics

consists of eleven words.

(Sorry, twelve.)

Or twenty if you include this.

An Empty Page

This page used to be empty
and liked it that way.
Enjoying its privacy,
staring out into space,
its face blank and expressionless.

Then we came along:
words!
Once we'd settled in,
readers soon followed,
all fingers and prying eyes.

As one of them,
how does it feel?
Guilty I hope.
This page used to be empty
and liked it that way.

Handwriting

From: Rowland Hill (R.H@royalmail.com)
Sent: October 2015
To: You
Subject: Handwriting

An email once sent, grows stale.
Bored in the inbox it will wither.

A letter well meant
is better

Stored in a tin box
it will last forever.

Freedom

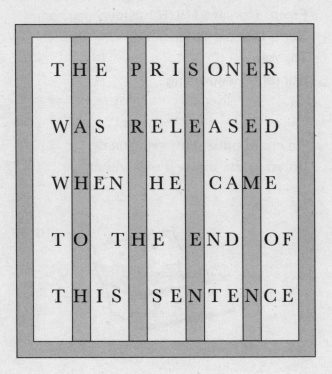

THE PRISONER
WAS RELEASED
WHEN HE CAME
TO THE END OF
THIS SENTENCE

First Blossoms

It must be spring.

In the garden suddenly

Reds, blues, pinks,

greens and yellows:

Slide

Sandpit

Trampoline

Paddling pool

Wheelbarrow

All excited and

raring to go.

Clerihews

To vaguely amuse

And banish the blues

Writing clerihews

I would choose.

***

Mr Merryhew

Would ferry you

Across the Thames at Bray

On a tea tray.

Mr Bland

On the other hand

Felt safer on land.

This I can well understand.

***

A pirate known as 'Lucky' Frank

Caught robbing the captain's piggy bank

Was about to walk the plank

When the ship sank.

Sunset and Custard

At the end of a hot day

The sun is an orange jelly

Still runny.

But you can bet

Come supper time

It will have set.

The Joke is on Us

The sun is a joker
Who likes having fun
Especially when
His work is done.

He pins up a notice
At the end of the day
Saying 'Moon',
Then, winking, slips away.

Alternative Santa

'I'm fed up looking like Father Christmas,'
Muttered Father Christmas one year.
'I need a new outfit. I must move with the times.
So, for a start, it's goodbye, reindeer.'

He googled 'alternative Santas'
And was amazed at the stuff that appeared.
He got rid of the holly-red costume,
Had a haircut, and shaved off his beard.

Spent weeks in front of a computer
In a cave hollowed out of the ice
Wearing a T-shirt emblazoned HAPPY HOLIDAY
And jeans (Amazon, half price).

Couldn't wait to straddle his snow-ped
(The bargain he'd bought on eBay):
A rocket-powered silver toboggan,
His supersonic sleigh.

Then one morning he thought, 'Oh why bother
Delivering presents by hand
When it could all be done online?
Busy parents will understand.

We are lucky to live in a digital age
Where the aim is access and speed.
SantaNet I'll call the system –
Santafaction guaranteed.'

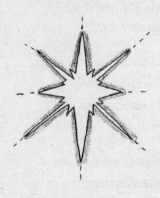

And that was years and years ago
Now little children barely know
About Midnight mass and mistletoe
Christmas carols and candle glow
Sleigh bells ringing across the snow
And Santa singing Yo ho ho
For that was years and years ago
For that was years and years ago.

Bad Queen Wenceslas

Wenceslas, who lived in the tenth century, was a good
man and a wise ruler. However, he was murdered
by his younger brother, Boleslav, who succeeded him
to the throne of Bohemia. Or did he . . .?

Good King Wenceslas looked out
On the feast of Stephen,
When the snow lay round about,
Deep and crisp and even.

Brightly shone the moon that night,
Though the frost was cruel,
When a poor man came in sight
Gathering winter fuel.

'Hither, page, and stand by me,
If thou know'st it, telling,
Yonder peasant who is he,
Where and what his dwelling?'

'Sire, he lives a good league hence,
Underneath the mountain,
Right against the forest fence
By St Agnes' fountain.'

Queen Wenceslas looked out of bed.
'Stupid old king,' Her Majesty said.
'Hanging out of the window on a frosty night,
The right royal bottom, not a pleasant sight.

'Thinks he sees an old man gathering fuel,
Wenceslas, alas, is a fool.
That's no peasant, that's his brother,
Who seeks the throne. Boleslav, my lover.

'Disguised as a pauper his plan is to lure
The king from his castle and ensure
That he follows him into the wood
Where the snow will purple with his blood.

'The royal page, disloyal, is in my pay
And paid to help my lover slay
Incywincy Wenceslas.
I wish this day would quickly pass.'

And pass it did but painful slow
With a body buried beneath the snow
And a wicked queen banished forever.
For page and monarch stood together.

For page and monarch stood together
In the cruel and frosty weather.
Side by side in the wood they fought
For loyalty earned cannot be bought.

And Boleslav lies a good league hence,
Underneath the mountain,
Right against the forest fence
By St Agnes' fountain.

The Brush Baby

The brush baby lives under the stairs
On a diet of dust and old dog hairs

In darkness dreading the daily chores
Of scrubbing steps and kitchen floors

Doomed to a life of fighting grime
The poor little wooden porcupine.

A Pair of Porcupines

Rolled up
Like a ball of twine
This porcupine is feeling fine
After a supper of pickles
Pork pies and port wine.

Supine
This porcupine
Is none too perky
After scoffing the remains
Of last year's Christmas turkey.

Hedgehog Soup

Why are the hedgehogs cock-a-hoop?

Because they know there's no demand

for hedgehog soup.

Here Come the Dinner Ladies

Here come the dinner ladies . . . *One Two Three*.
There's one meal for you and another for me.

> For you, there's . . .
> *Sausages floating in custard,*
> *Boiled cabbage, sardines and peas,*
> *Spider legs with onions,*
> *Deep fried, and covered with cheese.*
> (Enjoy.)

Here come the dinner ladies . . . *One Two Three*.
There's one meal for you and another for me

> For me, there's . . .
> *Roast chicken and chips,*
> *A pizza, freshly made,*
> *Ice cream with chocolate sauce*
> *And loads of lemonade.*
> (Yum yum.)

Here come the dinner ladies . . . *One Two Three*.
My granny, my mum and my Aunty Dee.

Poetry Pie

Newly baked and fresh today
Eat while hot or take away.

Poetry Pie, Poetry Pie
Straight from the oven our Poetry Pie.
Poetry Pie, Poetry Pie
We're all lovin' our Poetry Pie.

Rhymes and rhythms, raps and riddles.
No nonny-noes or hey-diddle-diddles.

Poetry Pie, Poetry Pie
We can't get enough of our Poetry Pie.
Poetry Pie, Poetry Pie
Lovin' the stuff in our Poetry Pie.

Poems that tickle and trip off the tongue.
Poems to be whispered, shouted and sung.
Poems that chuckle and poems that bite.
Poems that moan and go bump in the night.
Poems that meow and bark and roar.
Look out! Here comes a dinosaur . . .

Poetry Pie, Poetry Pie
There's nothing as nice as Poetry Pie.
Poetry Pie, Poetry Pie
Have a slice of our Poetry Pie.

Poems that stand apart from the crowd.
Poems that will make you laugh out loud.
Poems that go 'Wheee!' and jump off the shelf.
Poems that you'll want to keep to yourself.
Poems that you'll want to share with a friend.
Poems that you wish would never end.

Poetry Pie, Poetry Pie
Sing a song of Poetry Pie.
Poetry Pie, Poetry Pie
Ning Nang Nong, it's Poetry Pie.

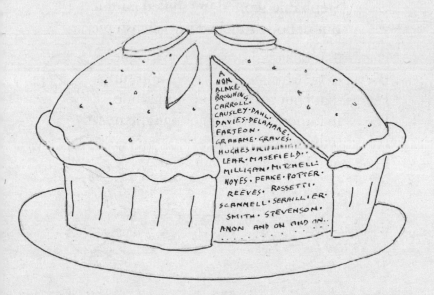

A
NON
BLAKE·
BROWNING
CARROLL·
CAUSLEY·DAHL·
DAVIES·DELAMARE·
FARJEON·
GRAHAME·GRAVES·
HUGHES·KIPLING·
LEAR·MASEFIELD·
MILLIGAN·MITCHELL·
NOYES·PEAKE·POTTER·
REEVES·ROSSETTI·
SCANNELL·SERRAILLIER·
SMITH·STEVENSON·
ANON AND ON AND ON··

Jellyfish Pie

Shuna chewed my tuna sandwich
Molly demolished my cucumber bap
Kylie slyly nibbled my bagel
Gavin unravelled my Mexican wrap

Betty bit my bacon butty
Gupta gulped my hard-boiled egg
Patsy pinched my crusty pasty
Nigella gnawed my chicken leg

Lisa licked my slice of pizza
Nicola nicked my shrimp on rye
Stephanie scoffed my stuffed panini
But nobody touched my jellyfish pie.

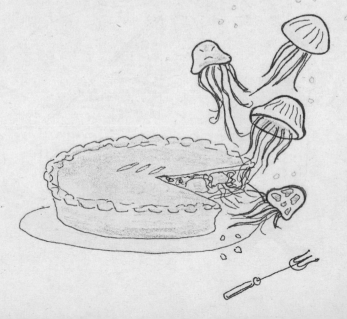

A Slice of Pie

(traditional rhyme)

How's your wife, your trouble and strife?
Thin as a knife, I cannot deny.
Can she eat a slice of pie?
She surely can, and so can I.

Served with custard sweet and hot
(although the pie is chicken?)
She'll eat the lot as sure as not
and the plate she'll keep a-lickin'.

Once Bitten

Nettles sting if you touch them.
It's their way of saying 'Good day.'
But I've no wish to befriend them
So I tend to keep well away

But if you're unlucky and get nettled
And a rash and blisters appear
Don't panic, no need to get rattled
The antidote is sure to be near

A dock leaf applied and amazing!
The pain will disappear fast
You're soon on your way and praising
Mother Nature's Elastoplast.

Tasty Bouquets

Cauliflowers are the perfect flowers
To give Mum on Mother's Day.
Covered with lots of grated cheese
She would cook them right away.

*

And elderflowers for grandma
Would really make her day
For though she may be elderly
She loves a sweet bouquet.

A Nice Fish Wish

Yesterday at supper time
While I was eating fish
I thought about the fishermen
And made a little wish.

To those who daily risk their lives
Amid gales and icy foam
I wish them bulging nets
Then a nice cup of tea at home.

The Fate of the Chip

From the plate

to the hip

via the lip.

Short trip.

La Vie d'une Pomme Frite

De l'assiette

A la bouche

Whoosh!

Couch Potato

This is the life for me:
Eating crisps while watching TV.

I lick my lips, snooze and slouch
On my baked, organic potato couch.

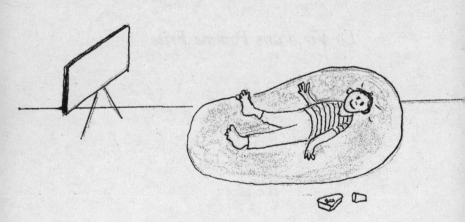

Patterns

Chips need ketchup
Or mayo on the side
So they can make patterns
Around the plate as they slide.

The Baggy-bottomed Shadow

Something's happened to my shadow
It no longer seems to fit
It's gone ragged round the edges
And gets crumpled when I sit.

I took it off last Sunday
When I went swimming in the lake.
Perhaps someone in a hurry
Took my shadow by mistake

And left theirs.

It's all baggy round the bottom
And fuzzy round the top,
If you're the one who took it
Can we meet and do a swap?

Two Naughty Identical Dentists

Twin brothers shared a surgery.

One was Jimmy, the other, Sammy.

Jimmy liked his donuts sugary.

Sammy, jammy.

***

Coinci dentally

their teeth fell out on the same day.

Double whammy.

Toothy Grin

There's a girl in our class called Lola

Who drinks nothing but sweet fizzy cola.

'Though I'm certain to burst

I've still got a thirst

And I'm left with only one molar.'

My Name is Ella

For E. D.

My name is Ella, not Ellie

Not Bella or Nelly

Stella or Kelly

Not Fenella, Nigella

Cinderella, Marcella

Priscilla or Shelly

Not Gorilla or Jelly

Umbrella or Belly.

My name is Ella, OK?

It was Holly

Was it Helen who looked like a film star?
Was it Gwen who stood out from the crowd?
The one I remember is Holly,
who made me laugh out loud.

Was it Janet who sang like an angel?
And Sophie who danced with such grace?
The one I remember is Holly,
who brought a smile to my face.

Was it Polly who sent my first valentine?
Or Molly her identical twin?
The one I remember is Holly
who made me giggle and grin.

I loved them all dearly when I was a boy
But I remember most clearly
the one who brought joy.

Besotted

A river's what an otter loves
But what an otter needs
Is another otter to play with
And potter about in the reeds.

To make water slides and diving pools
And dams to flood the banks.
Utterly besotted with otters,
When I spot otters I give thanks.

Famous

Excuse me, I'm famous.
Don't you recognize my face?
I've been in lots of famous groups
And appeared all over the place.

I've written lots of famous songs
And recorded lots of tunes.
I played all kinds of instruments
From saxophones to spoons.

You must know me, I was famous.
The one with the cheeky face
In a very famous boy band
That vanished without trace.

We played the famous festivals.
We were never off TV.
If I let you have my autograph,
Will you lend me 50p?

The Giant Finger

Walter was fed up. Not a minute's peace in years.
At the circus or enjoying a ride on the fairground
when suddenly: 'There's Wally!' On a crowded beach
or checking in at the airport: 'There's Wally!'
A giant finger crushing him into the ground.

Of course, Walter had tried to escape.
Even travelled back through time.
But a giant finger would wriggle its way
through a hole in history. 'I've found him!
There's Wally!' Finally he could take no more.

The bobble hat, rucksack and walking stick
he gave to Oxfam. The red-and-white striped jersey
he burned. With the money he made from the sale
of the snorkel, camera and binoculars he bought
contact lenses and a range of disguises.

He found an ordinary job in an ordinary town
but lives in constant fear of someone shouting
'Where's Wally?' and Walter shouting 'I'm here!'
After a menacing silence, comes the dreadful sound
of a giant finger pointing, then crushing him into the ground.

The Juggler

Cousin Amos,
Famous in his day,
Would only juggle with objects
Beginning with A

Like Acorns, Apples and Anchovies,
Alarm clocks, Armadillos and Armchairs
And, just the once, an Alligator,

Which, sad to say
Went straight for the jugular.

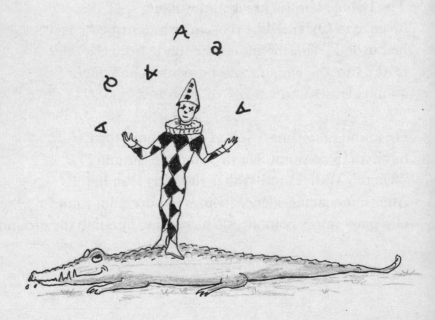

Defeat

Paint the goalposts black. Lower
the corner flags and fly them at halfmast.
Our team defeated and outclassed.

Weak in defence and attack. Our
supporters openly break down and weep.
Football legends, long dead, stir in their sleep.

Return the lions to their cages. Blow
the final whistle and play 'The Last Post'.
Then raise your glass and drink a toast . . .

To what might have been.

As Young as You Feel

I'd be the first to swim the Channel in pyjamas
The first to climb Mount Everest upside down
The first to cross the vast Saharan desert
On a tightrope dressed as a circus clown.

I'd be the first to win the Ladies Open Doubles
At Wimbledon, at tennis, on my own
The first to catch a fierce and mighty dragon
Whose roar is now the ringtone on my phone.

I'd be the first to surf Down Under underwater
On the belly of a hammer-headed shark
Race an alligator up an escalator
Go camping with vampires after dark.

I'd be the first to skateboard to the South Pole
South polar bears all marvelling at my skill.
The first to hang-glide all the way to Venus
And get back quick, because it's all downhill.

I'd be the first to leapfrog Blackpool Tower
Clear Grand Canyon in one almighty leap
Dream about the FA Cup at Wembley
Score the winning goal while walking in my sleep.

I'd be the first in all these things
So it's sad to reveal
That maybe now I'm past it
(Though they say you're as young as you feel).

Roger McGough (97½)

The One and Lonely

Everybody wishes they were me.
Who doesn't get out of bed every morning
Look in the mirror and, yawning,
Wish they were me instead?

Everybody wishes they were me.
I can tell by the way they keep their distance.
Out of respect, without a doubt,
I enter a room and they all walk out.

Everybody wishes they were me.
Afraid that they might bore me,
People turn their backs,
Lower their voices and ignore me.

But what they're thinking I can guess.
Alone and envious, they confess:
'Compared to him and his success
We are dross, a lumpen mess.

We lack his elegance, his finesse,
His cool, his style, his sense of dress.
A demi-god, no less. Yes,
If only we were he. If only we were he.'

You Are as Useless

'You are as useless,' he shouted
At the top of his lungs,

'As a cup without a handle
As a ladder without rungs

As a wick without a candle
A bicycle without a brake

As barbed wire without the barbs
A Scottish monster without a lake

As a potato without the carbs
A smoothie without the fruit

As a sporran without the kilt
A football lace without the boot

As a stilt walker without a stilt
A drummer without his sticks

As a playground without the slide
As a clock run out of ticks.

You are as useless,' he cried,
'As a cold, unbuttered scone

As a poem that goes on
And on and on and on . . .'

Lord of the Rungs

When our windows are mucky
They soon let us know.
'Our faces need cleaning,
Better send out for Joe.'

Lest our neighbours complain
(One or two can be sniffy)
We send out for Joe
Who is round in a jiffy.

With his chamois and his squeegee,
His cheesecloth and his scrim,
In the whole of streaky-window land
No one can rival him.

His bucket-balancing act
Draws applause from passers-by
As he climbs his dad's old ladder
Reaching up into the sky.

Where he stays like Sherpa Tensing
On the topmost rung
Till all the windows sparkle
And his final song is sung.

And to be fair to Joe
He doesn't suffer from vertigo.

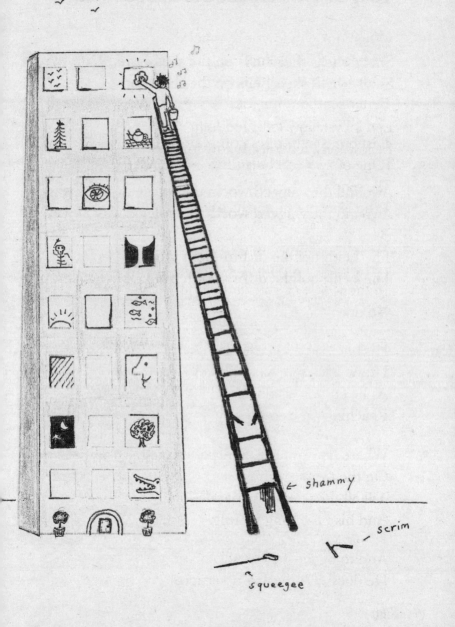

← shammy

← scrim

squeegee

Tongue Twisters for the Tongue-tied

Shally shells sheashells on the sheashore
Shally shells sheashells on the sheashore

Led lolly, lellow lolly, led lolly,
Lellow lolly, led lolly, lellow lolly

Awound the wugged wocks the wagged wascal wan
Awound the wugged wocks the wagged wascal wan

The Leith polithe dithmitheth uth
The Leith polithe dithmitheth uth

My Name is Izzy

My name is Izzy
Not Lizzie or Dizzy
Not Whizzy or Fizzy
Definitely not
Frizzy, Tizzy or Zizzy.

Easy to say
And easy to spell
My name is Izzy
(Though known at home as Isabel).

Skywriting

Clouds are the Earth's handwriting.

I open the sky

And don't like what I'm reading.

Lightning...

Tornado...

Hurricane...

Clouds are Post-its

Clouds are Post-its
Stuck on to the sky
Will the weather tomorrow
Be wet or dry?

Yesterday one was yellow
The rest were all blue
The message was clear
The sun's shining through

But today they're jumbled
Crumpled and grey
Meaning 'Bring your umbrellas
Rain's on the way.'

The Red Carpet

The handsome young man on the red carpet,
smiling at the cameras, waving to the crowd
and signing autographs, isn't me.
I am the red carpet.

I could easily have been the star,
one of the cameras, even an autograph.
However, as producer of the poem,
I have chosen to be the red carpet.

Such is the power of poets.

EYEBROWS

My brows are superior to your brows.

Eyebrows should wiggle and shine.

Yours are more like snail trails,

Mice tails, compared with mine.

EYE to EYE

Put two mirrors

Face to face

And unblinking

They'll outstare

Each other

Into eternity.

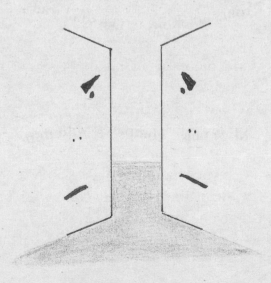

Nightmares

Even Big Bad Wolves have nightmares
Tossing and turning in their sleep
The invasion of the zombie rabbits
The attack of the sabre-toothed sheep.

Even alligators have nightmares
Grinding their teeth in bed.
The dentist saying,'They're all coming out.
From now on it's milk-soggy bread.'

Vampires have similar nightmares
About having lost their bite
And being lost in a hall of mirrors
Then waking to perpetual light.

Even dinosaurs had nightmares
(Their demise, alas, a mystery)
About ending up as skeletons
In museums of natural history.

Even your mum has nightmares
And one of them actually came true
The one about having a baby
And the baby turned out to be YOU!

Mirror Images

Hand Mirror

'My, what a handsome hand,'
Trilled the princess,
Admiring it in the hand mirror.

Rear-view Mirror

It is difficult
To get a good view
of your bottom
In a mirror.

The Wicked Queen's Mirror

Here she comes:
'Mirror, mirror on the wall,
who is the fairest of them all?'
One of these days, just for a joke,
I'll say 'Dopey' and watch her choke.

The Cracked Mirror

It came as a shock
But I live in hope.
A new life beckons
As a kaleidoscope.

On Reflection

When a mirror looks in the mirror
Does it like what it sees?
Mirrors, on reflection,
Are easy to please.

Fairground Mirrors

If fat, I make you look thin.
Thin? I make you look fat.

Never trust a mirror.
Simple as that.

School for Ghouls

I am where they come to practise.
Those ghosts and vampires
who disturb you in the middle of the night.

On me they rehearse the dark arts
of spreading goosebumps and panic
Put on their masks in the fading light.

I am where they come to learn
how to break and enter dreams,
Fix their make-up and hone their skills.

On me they test their moans and screams.
Roll their eyes, pull ugly faces.
Perfect the chases, and the kills.

I am where the headless warm up,
Where skeletons work out,
Demons and monsters run free.

Those actors who scare so well
in your nightmares
have all practised first on me.

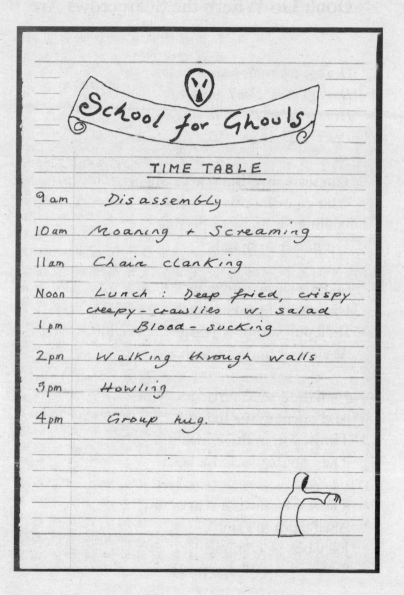

School for Ghouls

TIME TABLE

9 am	Disassembly
10 am	Moaning + Screaming
11 am	Chair clanking
Noon	Lunch : Deep fried, crispy creepy-crawlies w. salad
1 pm	Blood-sucking
2 pm	Walking through walls
3 pm	Howling
4 pm	Group hug.

Don't Go Where the Scarecrows Are

Don't go where the scarecrows are.
Don't go there. Don't go there.
Don't go where the scarecrows are.
Don't go. Don't go . . .

The scarecrow is a scary crow
Who guards a private patch,
Waiting for an unsuspecting
Trespasser to snatch.

Stuffing straw into your mouth,
His twiggy fingers scratch.
He'll pull you down upon the ground
As circling birdies watch.

He'll drag you to his hidey-hole
And open up the hatch.
Throw you to the crawlies
Then double-lock the latch.

The scarecrow is a scary crow
Always out to catch
Juicy bits of compost
To feed his cabbage patch.

So don't go where the scarecrows are.
Don't go there. Don't go there.
Don't go where the scarecrows are.
Don't go. Don't go . . .

Don't go where the scarecrows are.
Don't go there. Don't go there.
Don't go where the scarecrows are.
Don't go. Don't go . . .

The Scarecrow Replies

Another scary scarecrow verse.
Honestly, it's just not fair.
My reputation's such a curse.
It's birds I'm here to scare.

Not children or townsfolk
Out for a breath of fresh air.
Those horror stories are a joke.
It's birds I'm here to scare.

I didn't choose these ragged clothes,
Dirty straw instead of hair.
Why you're frightened, heaven knows.
It's birds I'm here to scare.

I can't help the way I'm made.
All I ask is be aware
That it's my job, don't be afraid.
It's birds I'm here to scare.

The Question

The witch impatient in her lair.

The dragon in its den.

The question little children fear

Is not If? But When?

Questions, Questions

Dad, Dad,
If the barber cuts off that man's ear,
can I have it?

Quiet, son, quiet.

Dad, Dad,
Does an octopus have four legs and four arms,
or is it the other way round?

Quiet, son, quiet.

Dad, Dad,
How much do bulls charge?

Quiet, son, quiet.

Dad, Dad,
Does a giraffe have a long neck because its
feet smell?

Quiet, son, quiet.

Dad, Dad,
What's the capital of seven times thirty-three?

Quiet, son, quiet.

Dad, Dad,
You don't mind me asking all these questions,
do you?

Of course not, son.
If you don't ask, you never learn.

Tomorrow Has Your Name on It

Tomorrow has your name on it
It's written up there in the sky
As you set out on a journey
In search of the How? and the Why?

Oh the people you'll meet
The bright and the mad
The sights to be seen
The fun to be had.

Oh the dreams that you'll dream
The chances you'll take
The prizes you'll win
The hands that you'll shake.

But don't let your dreams
Get too big for their boots
Don't hanker after the flimflam of fame
If you hunger for mere celebrity
You'll be drawn like a moth to the flame.

For having dreams is not enough;
You must get down and do your stuff.
Take the ready with the rough.
Ride the punches, and my hunch is
You'll succeed when life gets tough.

And it will!
(That's also written in the sky
In a cobwebby corner of the Milky Way
A squillion zillion miles away).

Bullies will want to bully you
For that's what bullies do
And you'll feel small and miserable
(Don't worry, I would too).

Even Big Bad Wolves have nightmares,
One of the reasons they howl at the moon.
Being scared is Nature's medicine.
Not nice, but it's over soon.

There'll be days you're made to feel foolish
When your head seems made out of wood
When you blush, mumble and shuffle
Feel embarrassed and misunderstood.

Things will get lost or stolen
Life doesn't turn out as you'd planned
You get sick and then you get better –
What's gone wrong? You can't understand.

Take your time.
Sing your own songs and laugh out loud.
Weep, if you need to
But away from the crowd.

Disappointments will ebb and flow
Like the tide upon the shore
But an angry storm will quickly go
And the sun rise up once more.

Oh the dreams that you'll dream
The promises you'll make
The friends that you find
Whom you'll never forsake.

Oh the dreams that you'll dream,
May the good ones come true.
Being young is an adventure
How I wish I were you.

Today is the tomorrow we worried about
Yesterday and all last night.
And as days go, as days they do.
It seemed to go all right.

So dream your dreams and journey
Be tomorrow foul or fine
So you can say at the end of it
'Amazing! Today was mine.'

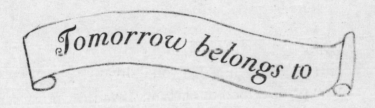

Tomorrow belongs to

Answers to 'The Game of Rhymes'

stingy
knobbly (a half-rhyme)
Scottie
humpy (or lumpy)
squawky
fangy
fish and chips*

*Macaroni would have been a clever answer but it is the wrong one. The answer is fish and chips because I like fish and chips and this is my poem.

Your Poetry Notebook

CUT OUT AND PASTE
INTO THE FRONT
OF YOUR POETRY NOTEBOOK

The funny things you overheard,
Write them down, every word.

Images, jokes, whopping great lies,
Storms in teacups, skies in pies.

Favourite lyrics, snatches of verse.
A prayer, a blessing, a spellbinding curse.

The misadventures, imagined or real.
Those puzzling dreams, the way that you feel.

This book wants to know what you have to say
So keep it handy and feed it each day.

Index of First Lines

'Roger McGough is a true original and more than
one generation would be much the poorer without
him' – *The Times Educational Supplement*

'. . . A collection that works well on the page
and is a delight to read aloud' – *Guardian*

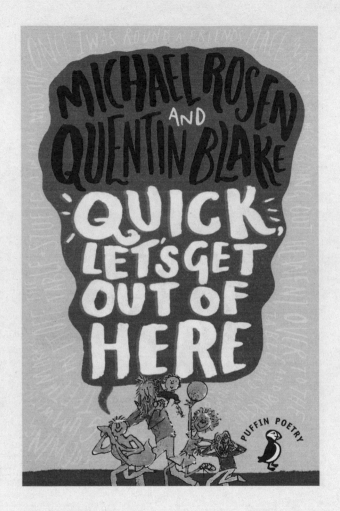

MICHAEL ROSEN AND QUENTIN BLAKE

'QUICK, LET'S GET OUT OF HERE'

PUFFIN POETRY

'Michael Rosen is one of our most popular writers – the champion for every bored, overdrilled, tested-to-tears pupil in the land' – *The Times*

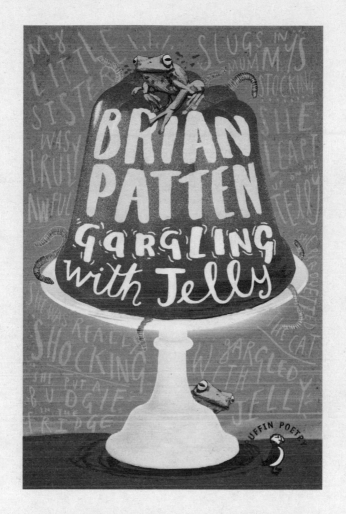

Full of Brian Patten's wonderful wit!

'Very silly, utterly crazy humour' – Jeremy Strong,
Guardian

A collection of witty and brilliant poems that
bring our monarchy to life!

It all started with a Scarecrow

Puffin is over seventy years old.
Sounds ancient, doesn't it? But Puffin has never been
so lively. We're always on the lookout for the next big
idea, which is how it began all those years ago.

Penguin Books was a big idea from the mind of
a man called Allen Lane, who in 1935 invented
the quality paperback and changed the world.
**And from great Penguins, great Puffins grew,
changing the face of children's books forever.**

The first four Puffin Picture Books were hatched in 1940 and the
first Puffin story book featured a man with broomstick arms called
Worzel Gummidge. In 1967 Kaye Webb, Puffin Editor, started the
Puffin Club, promising to **'make children into readers'**.
She kept that promise and over 200,000 children became devoted
Puffineers through their quarterly instalments of *Puffin Post*.

Many years from now, we hope you'll look back and
remember Puffin with a smile. **No matter what your age
or what you're into, there's a Puffin for everyone.**
The possibilities are endless, but one thing is for sure:
whether it's a picture book or a paperback, a sticker book
or a hardback, **if it's got that little Puffin
on it – it's bound to be good.**

www.puffinbooks.com